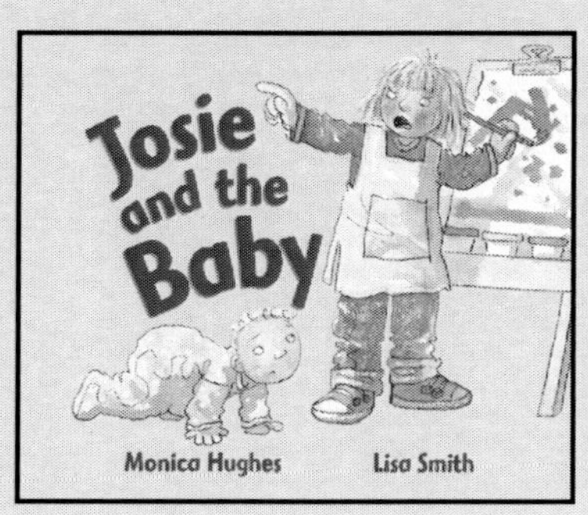

Walkthrough

This is another story about Josie.

Have you read any other stories about Josie? (e.g. *Josie and the Kite, Goodnight Josie,* and *Josie and the Junk Box*)

Let's read the title of this story together: 'Josie and the Baby'.

Josie is the girl in this picture.

What is happening?

Why is she pointing?

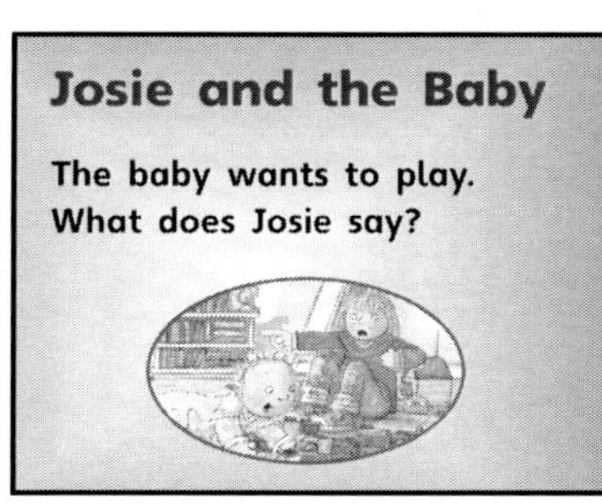

Walkthrough

Let's read the blurb together.

Do you think Josie is happy with the baby?

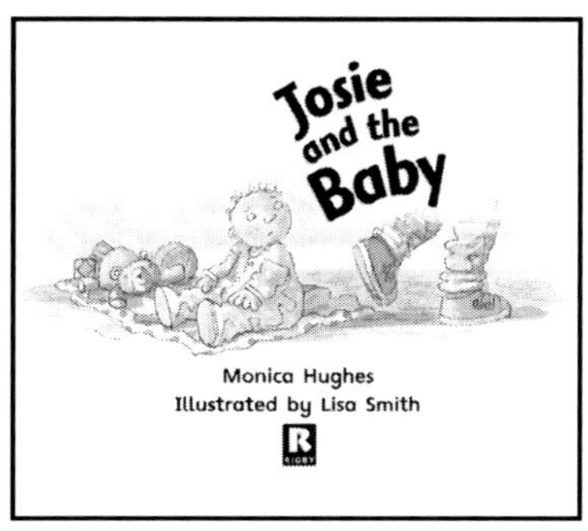

Walkthrough

Let's read the title again together: 'Josie and the Baby'.

How do you think the baby feels?

What do you think Josie did?

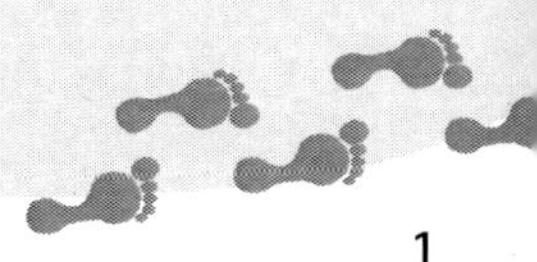

Look, Josie had a farm.

What did the baby want?

Yes, the baby wanted to play too.

Josie had a farm.
The baby wanted to play.

2

 **Observe and Prompt**

Word Recognition

- Check the children can read 'Josie'. If they have difficulty, model the reading of this word for them.

- Check the children are reading 'farm' and 'play' using their decoding skills.

- Check the children are using their decoding skills to read 'wanted'. If the children have difficulty with this word, ask them if they recognise the initial letter and sound, and model the blending of this word for them.

Observe and Prompt

Language Comprehension

- Ask the children what Josie had.
- Ask the children what the baby wanted to do.
- What do the children think Josie will say to the baby?

Walkthrough

Look, Josie's pointing again.

What do you think she said to the baby?

Josie said, "Go away, baby! Go away!"

4

 **Observe and Prompt**

Word Recognition

- Check the children can read 'away' and 'baby' using their decoding skills. Check they can hear the long 'a' sound in these words.

- Check the children can read the sight words 'said' and 'go'.

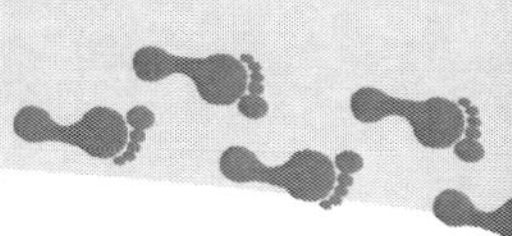

Observe and Prompt

Language Comprehension

- Prompt for expressive reading. Point out the exclamation marks and speech marks. Can the children make it sound like Josie is talking?

- Ask the children what Josie says to the baby.

- How do the children think Josie feels?

Walkthrough

What did Josie have?

Do you think the baby wanted to play with his own toys?

No, the baby wanted to play with the train.

Josie had a train.
The baby wanted to play.

6

 **Observe and Prompt**

Word Recognition

- Check the children can read 'train' using their decoding skills. You may need to help the children by modelling the reading of the 'ai' sound.

- Explain that the words 'train' and 'play' are spelled differently, but have the same long 'a' sound.

Observe and Prompt

Language Comprehension

- Ask the children what Josie had.
- Do the children think she likes the train?
- Ask the children what the baby wanted to do.
- Do the children think Josie will let the baby play?

Now Josie's cross again.

What do you think she said?

Josie said, "Go away, baby! Go away!"

8

Observe and Prompt

Word Recognition

● Check the children are reading 'Josie' more confidently.

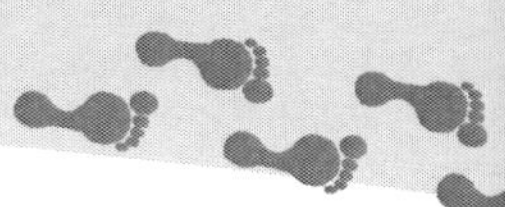

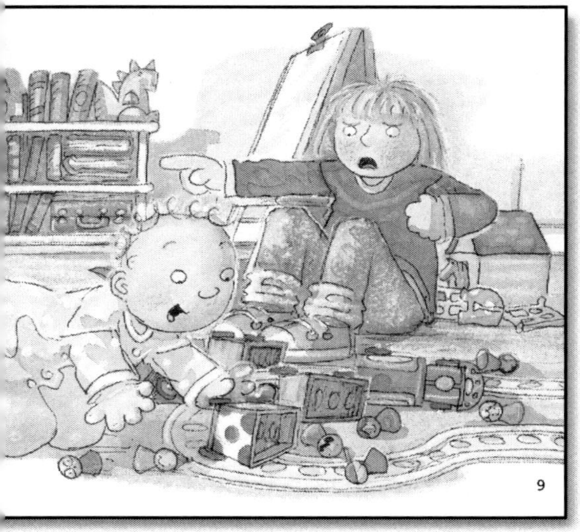

Language Comprehension

- Ask the children what Josie says.

- How do the children think she says it?

- Do the children think Josie likes the baby playing with her toys?

Walkthrough

Then Josie had some paints.

What happened next?

Yes, the baby wanted to play.

 **Observe and Prompt**

Word Recognition

- Check the children can read the sight word 'some'.
- Check the children can read the word 'paints'. If they have difficulty with this word, help them with the 'ai' sound.

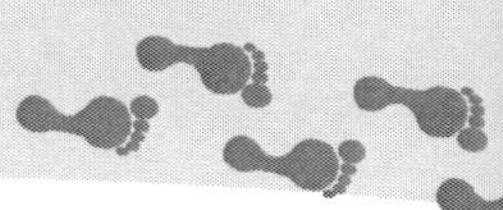

Observe and Prompt

Language Comprehension

- Ask the children what Josie had.
- Do the children think Josie will let the baby play?
- What do the children think Josie will say to the baby?

What do you think Josie told the baby?

Observe and Prompt

Word Recognition

- Check the children are more confident using their decoding skills to read 'away' and 'baby'.

Observe and Prompt

Language Comprehension

- If the children are not reading expressively, point out the exclamation marks and speech marks.

- How do the children think Josie feels?

- How do the children think the baby feels? How can they tell?

Walkthrough

Josie doesn't look cross now.

What did she have?

What do you think the baby wanted to do?

Point out the expression on the baby's face.

 **Observe and Prompt**

Word Recognition

- Check the children can read 'book' and 'look' using their decoding skills.
- Check the children can read the sight word 'to'.

What did Josie do next?

👁 Observe and Prompt

Language Comprehension

- Ask the children what the baby wanted to do.
- Do the children think Josie will let the baby look?
- What do the children think will happen next?

Walkthrough

Were you right?

Yes, Josie said the baby could come and look at the book.

 **Observe and Prompt**

Word Recognition

- Check the children can use their decoding skills to read 'Yes'.

Language Comprehension

- Prompt for expressive reading. Point out the speech marks.
- Ask the children what Josie said in the end.
- How do the children think the baby feels now?

16

Revisit and Respond

- Ask the children to read the story again to a partner making the talking even more expressive, i.e. making Josie sound really cross, and then really friendly on the last page. Check the children take account of punctuation to read with appropriate expression.

- Talk about the story setting and incidents and ask the children to relate them to their own experience.

- Divide the group into pairs and have each pair act out the story.

- Ask the children to spell the following words using magnetic letters: **train, paint, away, play**.

Independent Group Activity Work

This book is accompanied by two photocopy masters, one with a reading focus, and one with a writing focus, which support the teaching objectives of this book. The photocopy masters can be found in the Planning and Assessment Guide.

PCM F1.1 (*reading*)

PCM F1.2 (*writing*)

You may also like to invite the children to read the story again, during their independent reading (either at school or at home).

ASSESSMENT POINTS

Assess that the children have learnt the main teaching focus of the book by checking that they can:

Word Recognition	Language Comprehension
<ul><li>use their decoding skills when tackling new words</li><li>recognise and use alternative ways of spelling the long vowel sound 'ā' (e.g. in 'train' and 'play').</li></ul>	<ul><li>identify the main events of the story and relate them to their own experiences</li><li>comment on character feelings.</li></ul>

Josie and the Baby

Word Recognition Teaching Focus

- Strand 5: Recognise and use alternative ways of spelling the phonemes already taught, for example that the long vowel sound /ā/ can be spelt with 'ai' and 'ay'.

Language Comprehension Teaching Focus

- Strand 8: Visualise and comment on events, characters and ideas, making imaginative links to their own experiences.

Genre
Modern realistic story with a familiar family setting, two characters and patterned language

Story Summary
Josie was annoyed when the baby kept trying to join in with her activities. In the end, she found something they could both enjoy.

Children reading Yellow Level are working within level 1
They can:
- follow print with eyes, finger-pointing only at points of difficulty
- take note of punctuation to support the use of grammar and oral language rhythms
- cross-check all sources of information more quickly while reading
- notice relationships between one text and another
- predict in more detail.

To find out more about Rigby products, plus free supporting resources, visit

www.rigbyed.co.uk
01865 888020

ISBN 978-0-433049-33-3